FINGERPICKING GUITAR *Harp Style*

El McMeen
and
Sandy Shalk

I0810759

Online Audio

A computer generated audio file of each solo is available.
To access the online audio go to:
WWW.MELBAY.COM/31125MEB

Cover image is courtesy of Franklin Guitar Company.
Custom Dreadnaught made by Nick Kukich, Franklin Guitar Company.
Dyed red sugar maple back and sides with English Sycamore top.

Exclusive Sales Agent: Mel Bay Publications, Inc.
WWW.MELBAY.COM

Contents

Preface......3

The Music......6

Title	Page	Audio
In Christ There Is No East or West	6	1
Princess Royal	8	2
Captain O'Kain	12	3
Gentle Annie	16	4
The Mist-Covered Mountains of Home	20	5
Flow Gently, Sweet Afton	24	6
Casadh	28	7
Rose of Allendale	32	8
Once in a Blue Moon	36	9

Preface

This Mel Bay book covers a favorite topic of ours: playing guitar "harp style!" The harp can be played in many different ways, of course, but we are focusing on the approach of having notes flow from the instrument in an atmospheric and evocative way. We guitarists can do that by playing across the strings of the guitar, often in eighth notes and often using a form of "cross-picking," where we play successive melody notes on different strings. Classical guitarists call this "campanella fingering," or having a "campanella effect." (Campanella means "little bell," reflecting the bell-like sound that results from this technique.) We guitarists can use open and fretted strings. We sometimes opt for higher positions on lower strings. We can even play through harmonics and fretted notes to produce what is sometimes called "cascading harmonics." The point is to have appealing, flowing music that rings out.

Our book begins with an illustration of two possible approaches to a classic Christian hymn, "In Christ There is No East or West." The first is chordal; the second is harp style. The harp style technique has the beneficial effect, we think, of opening a piece of music with a strong quarter-note or on-the-beat vibe and creating an opportunity to explore different sonorities and rhythms, and melodic variations.

We don't want to overdo the atmospheric approach, however, and have notes ringing out all over the place. The melody might well get lost in a tonal soup. Harpers themselves disagree about the legitimacy or extent of letting their strings ring out, and many serious harpers are careful to damp vibrating strings so that the notes don't "bleed" into each other. We guitarists, moreover, have some important advantages over our harper brethren. We can sustain and color notes via fretting and vibrato techniques, and we can bend notes, slide in and out of notes, and employ unison notes (the same note being played simultaneously on different strings).

We have included our arrangements in various genres to show something of the breadth of the possibilities for playing harp style. Some of the pieces were originally harp tunes, composed by Turlough O'Carolan, who lived in Ireland from 1670 to 1738 ("Captain O'Kain" and "Princess Royal"). "Gentle Annie" is a Stephen Foster tune. "Casadh" (meaning "turn") is the traditional Irish melody used in the song "The Turning of the Road." The tune "Rose of Allendale" is an English song, with the melody by Sidney Nelson. "The Mist-Covered Mountains of Home" is a Scottish song, and "Flow Gently, Sweet Afton" is the melody by the American lawyer, composer, and pastor Jonathan Spillman supporting the Robert Burns poem. The book concludes with the masterpiece by Jerome Kern from 1923 called "Once in a Blue Moon," an arrangement that combines chordal and harp style playing. All the tunes are in Standard guitar tuning (EADGBE) or, in the case of "Casadh" and "Rose of Allendale," Drop D (DADGBE). It's very important that you follow the tablature, so that you can see the tuning, and our recommended fingerings.

We hope you enjoy our efforts here! Please feel free to share with us, via our websites, your own harp style explorations.

El and Sandy

NJ and Delaware

In Christ There is No East or West

In Christ There is No East or West (Page 2/2)

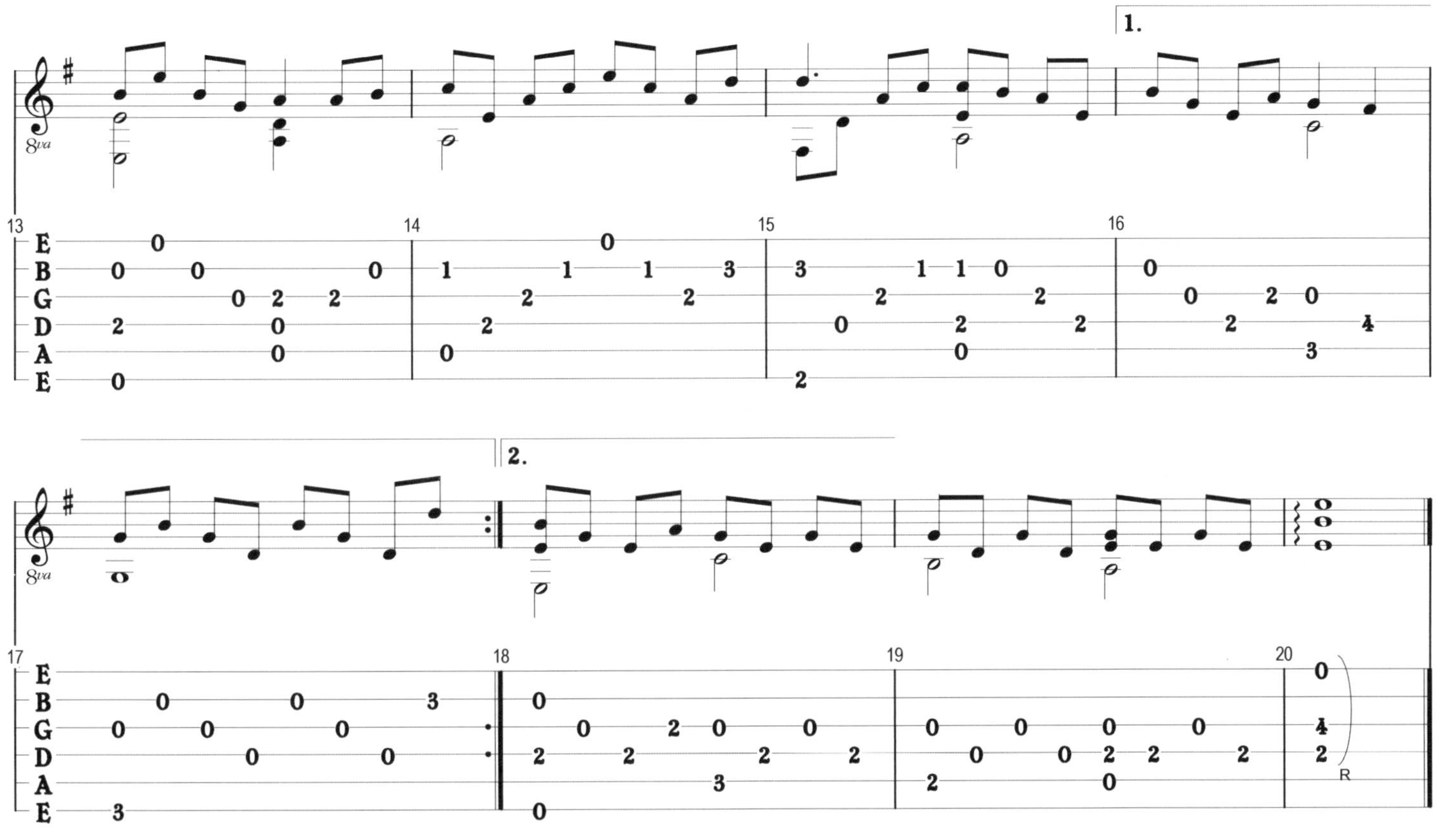

Princess Royal

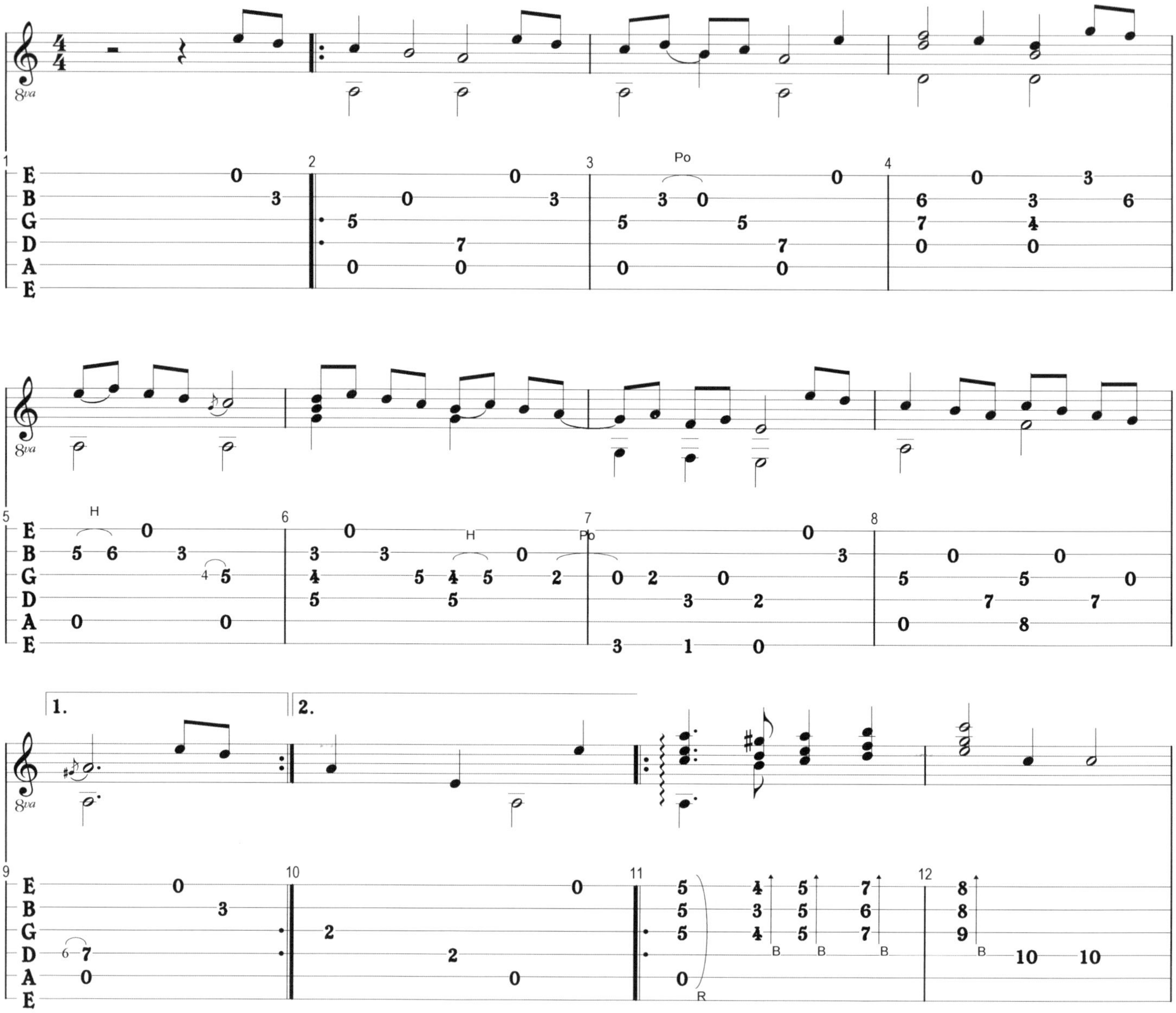

Princess Royal (Page 2/3)

8va
E
B
G
D
A
E
Po
H
B
R
1.
2.

Captain O'Kain

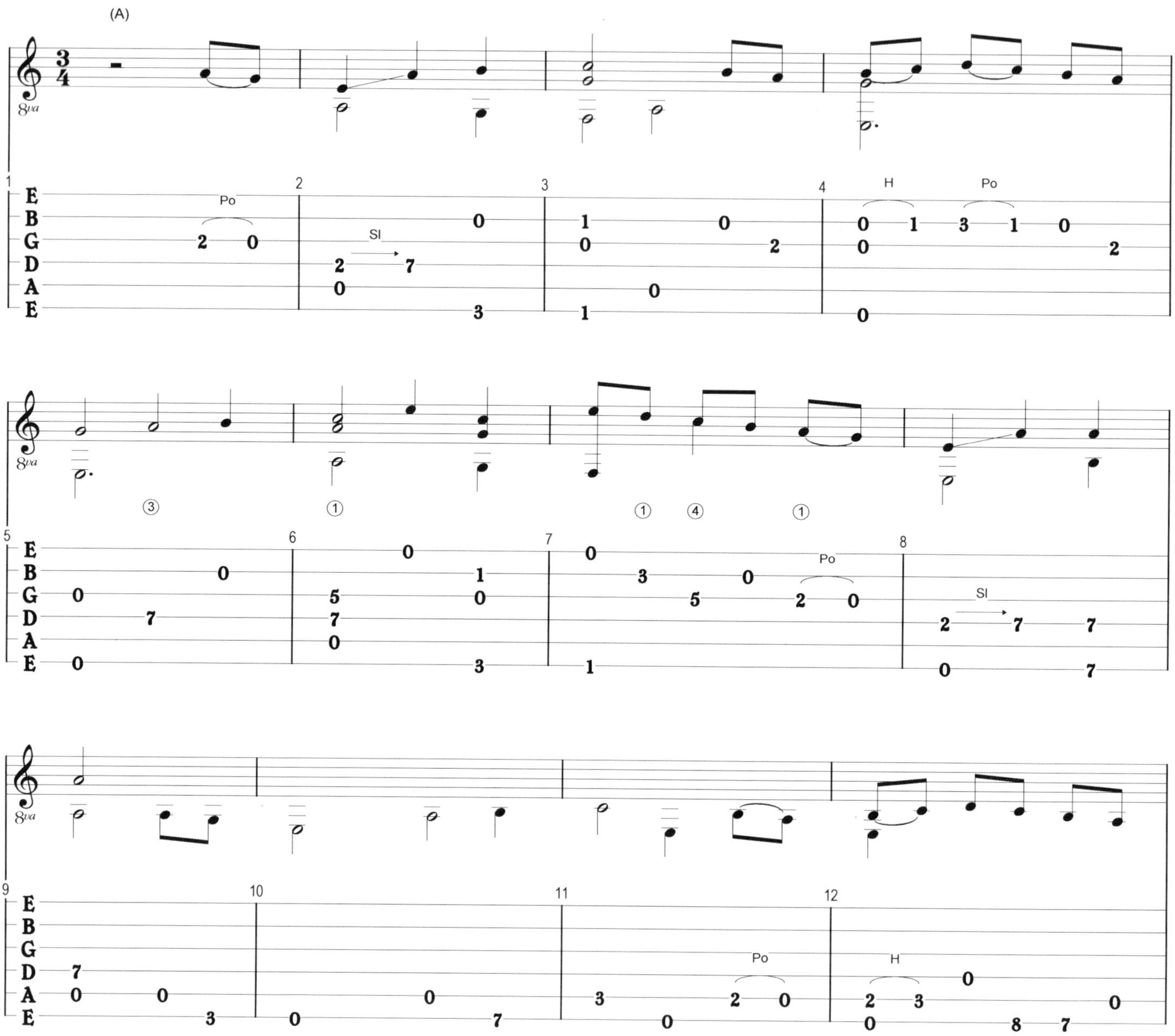

Captain O'Kain (Page 2/4)

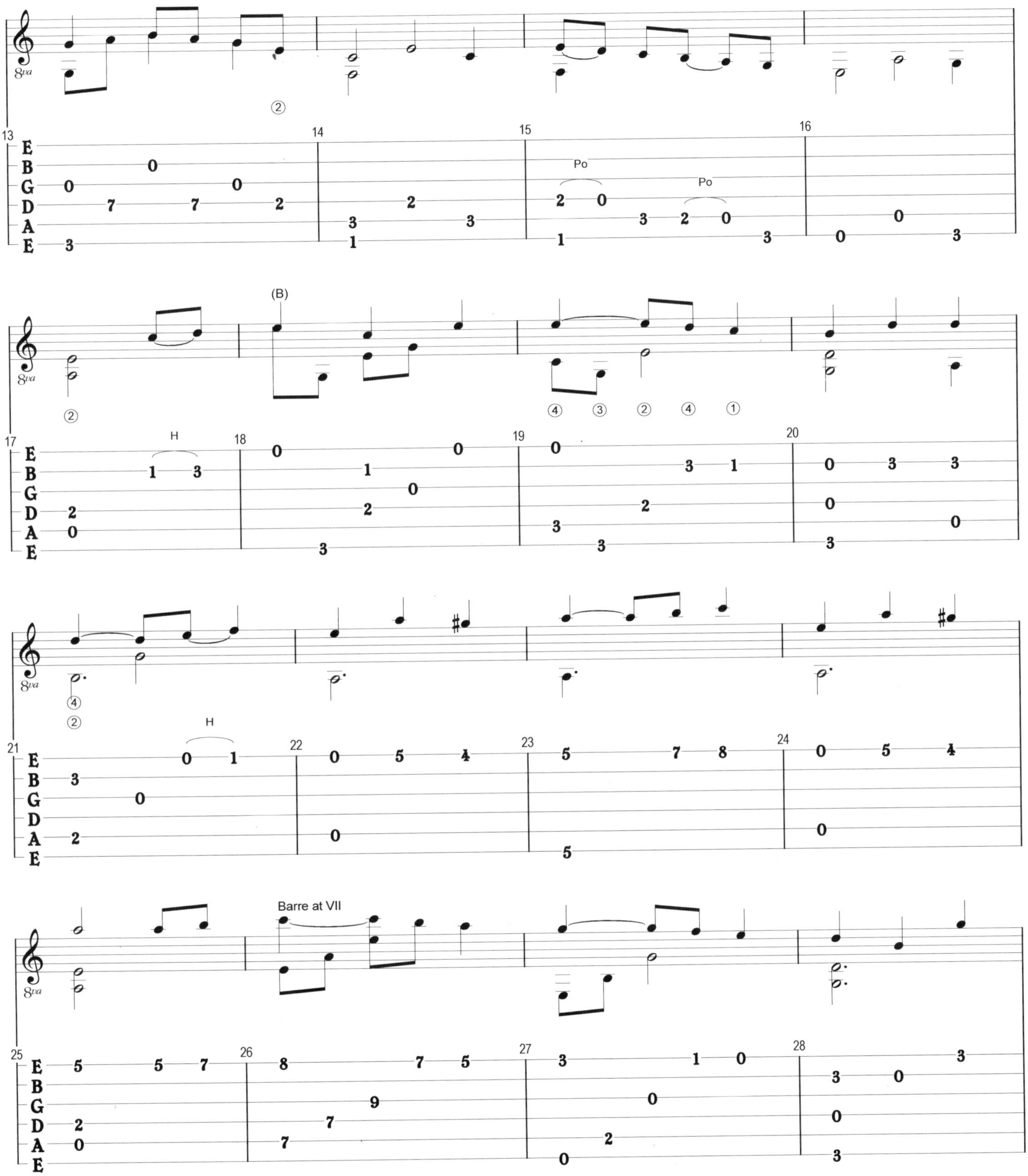

Captain O'Kain (Page 3/4)

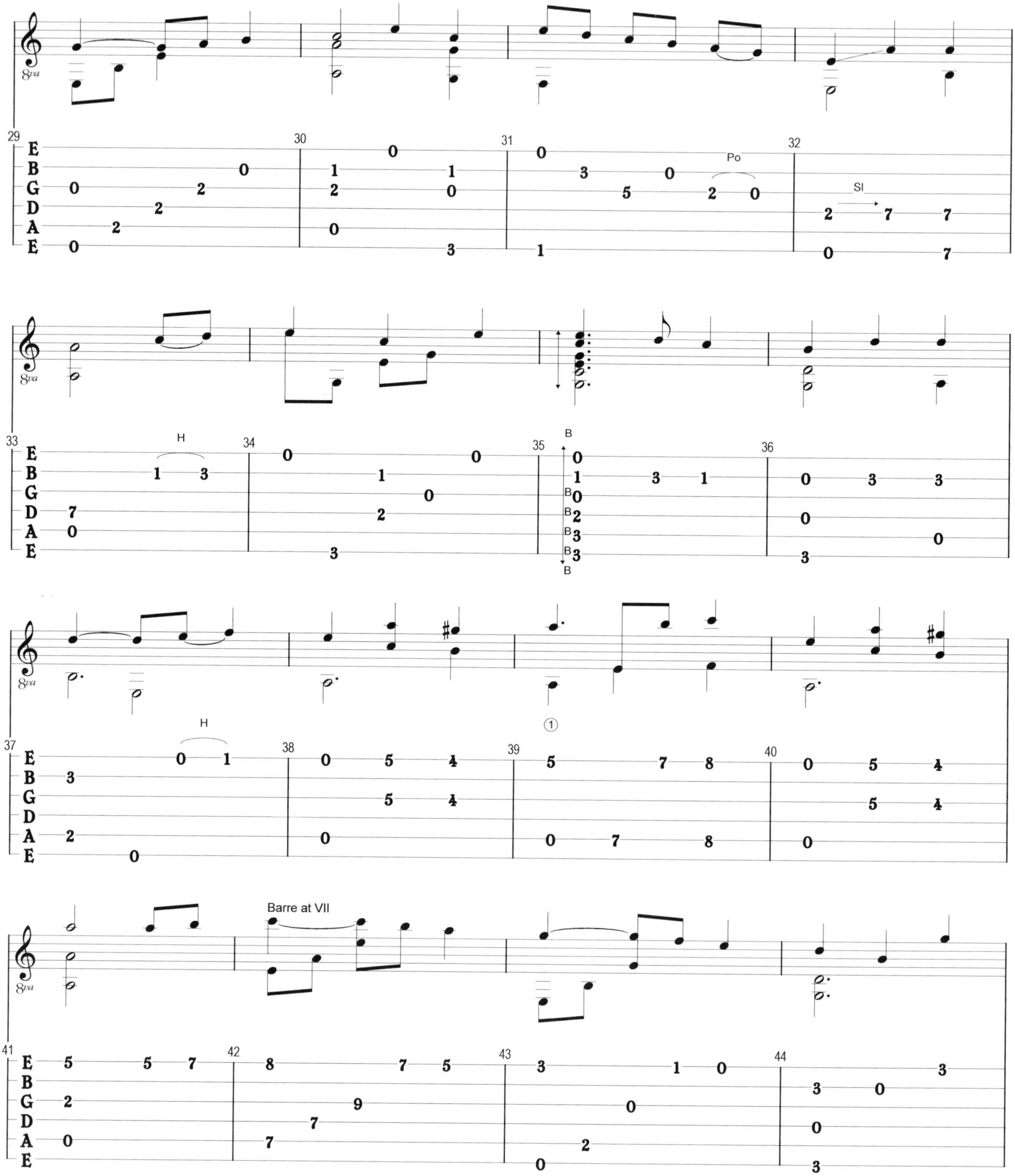

Captain O'Kain (Page 4/4)

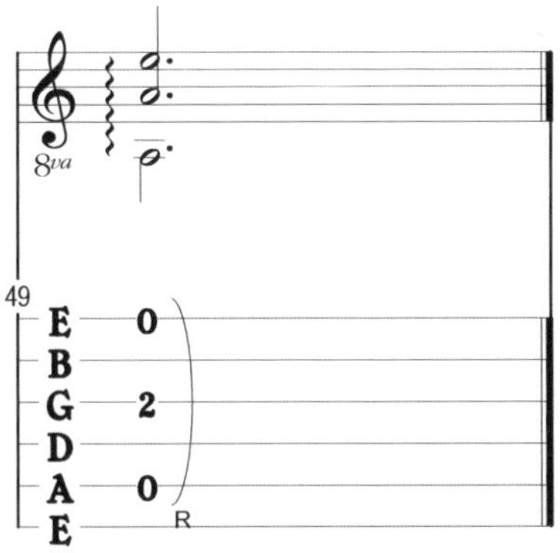

Gentle Annie

4

Gentle Annie (Page 2/3)

Gentle Annie (Page 3/3)

The Mist-Covered Mountains of Home

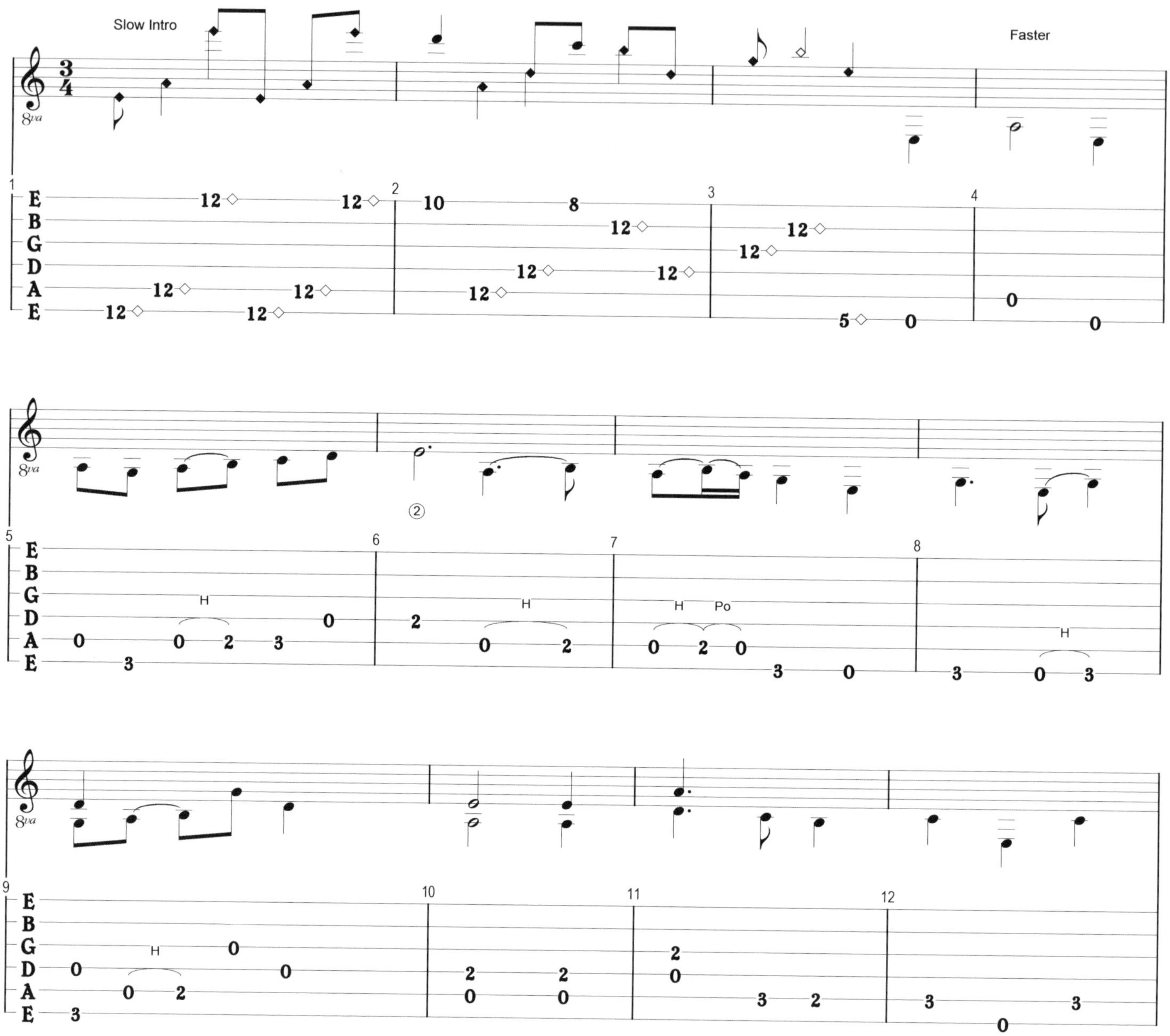

The Mist-Covered Mountains of Home (Page 2/4)

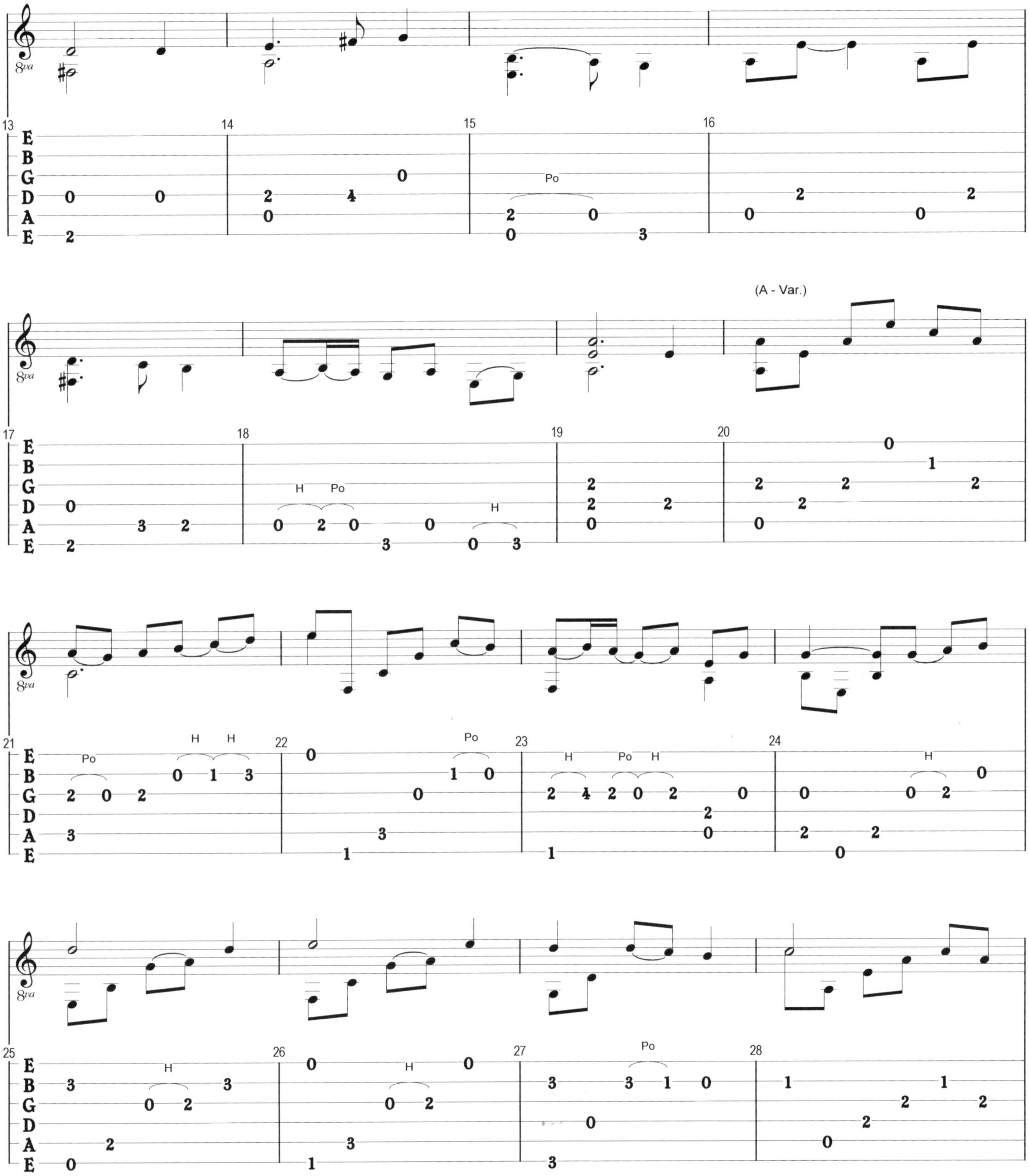

The Mist-Covered Mountains of Home (Page 3/4)

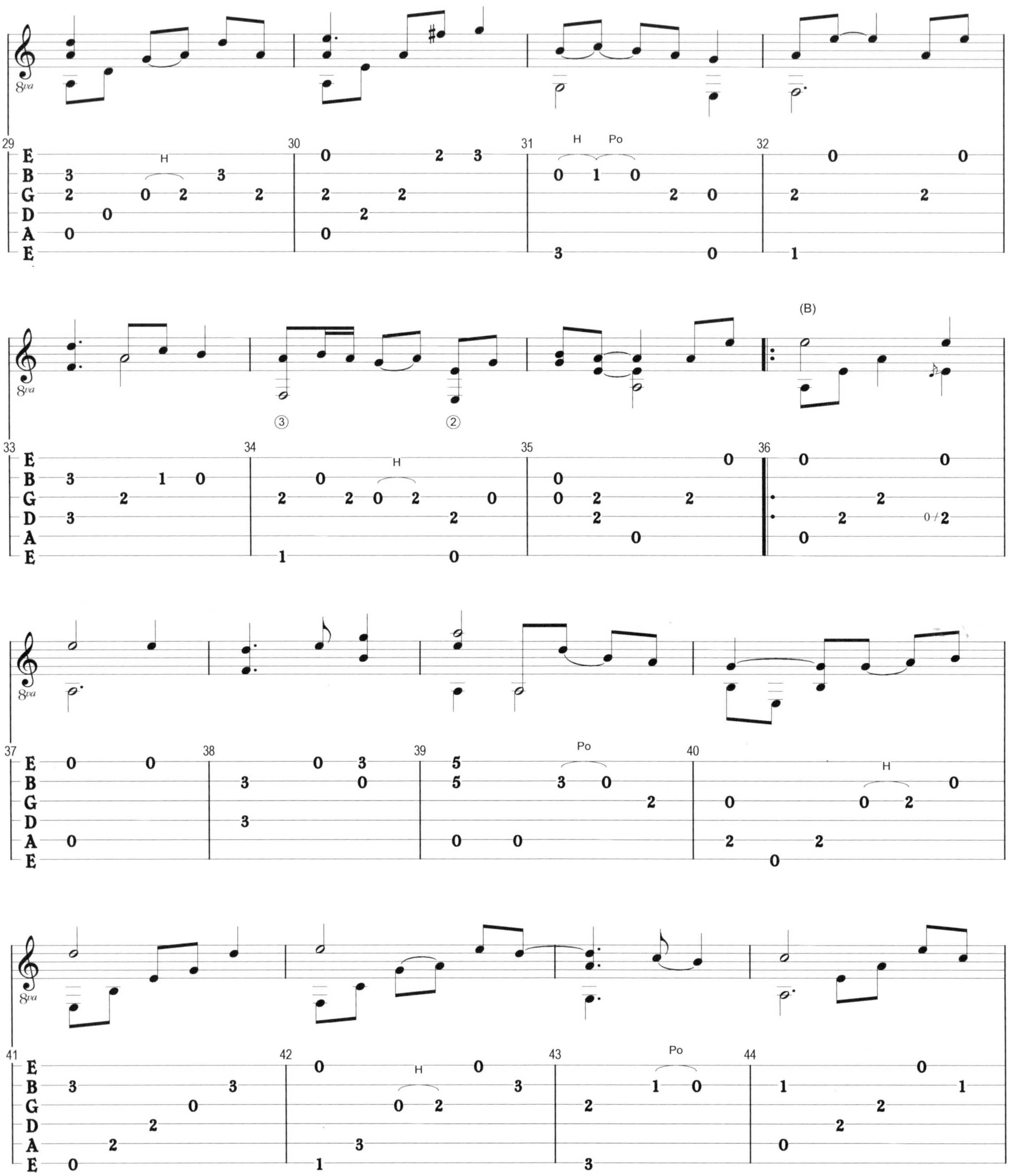

The Mist-Covered Mountains of Home (Page 4/4)

6

Flow Gently, Sweet Afton

Flow Gently, Sweet Afton (Page 2/3)

Flow Gently, Sweet Afton (Page 3/3)

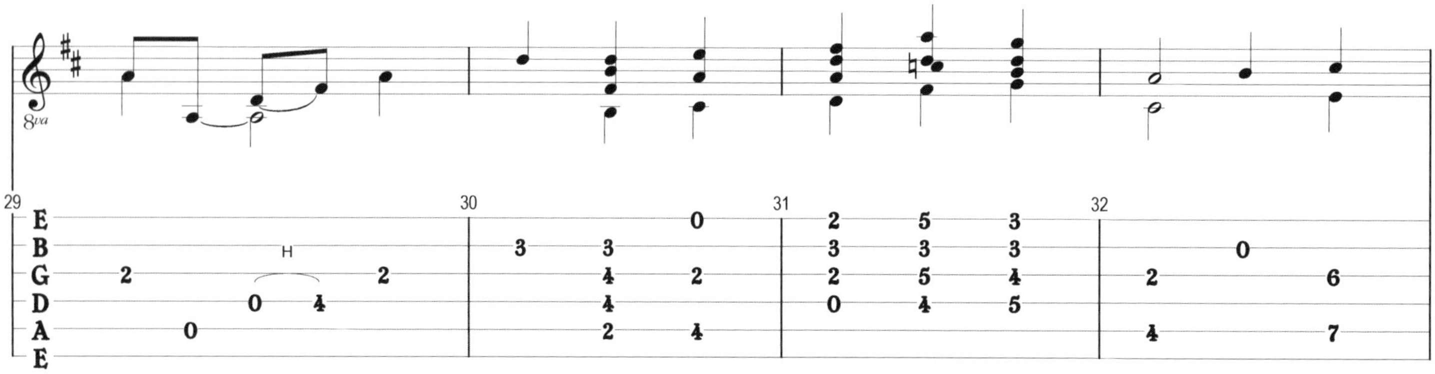

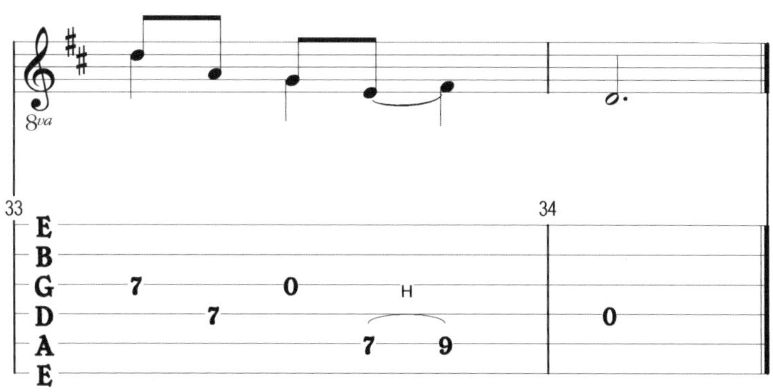

Casadh

Dropped-D Tuning

Casadh (Page 2/4)

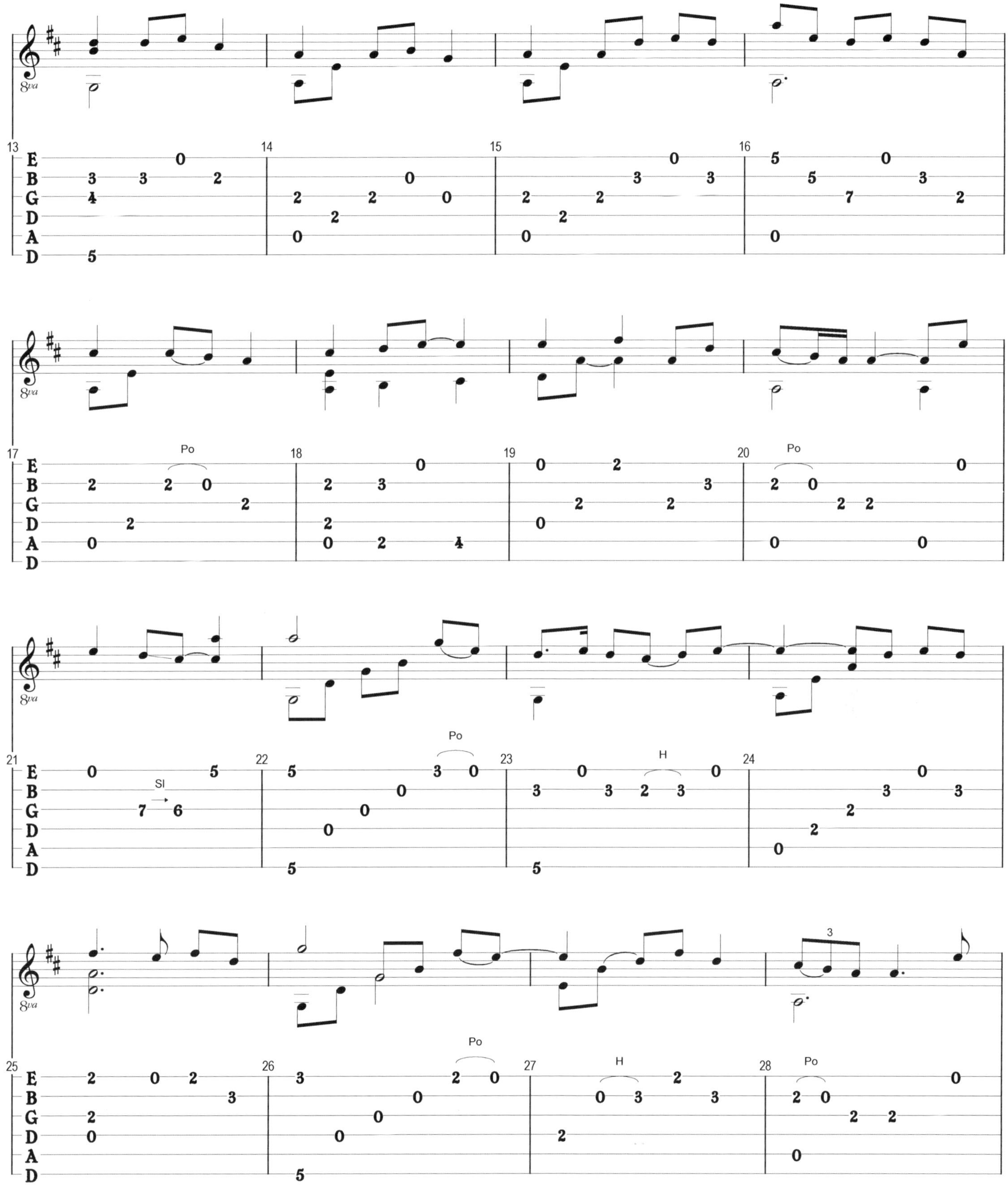

Casadh (Page 3/4)

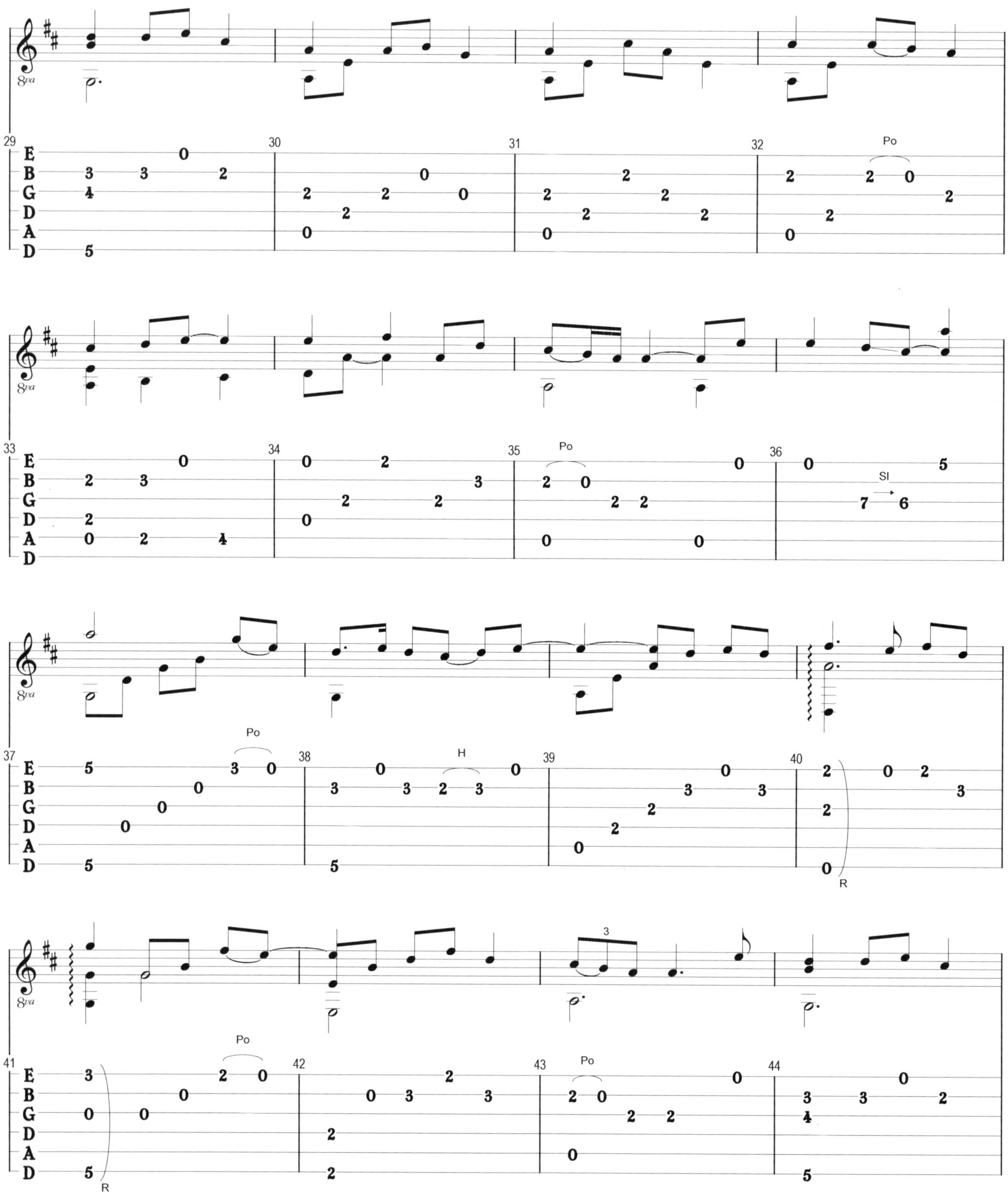

Casadh (Page 4/4)

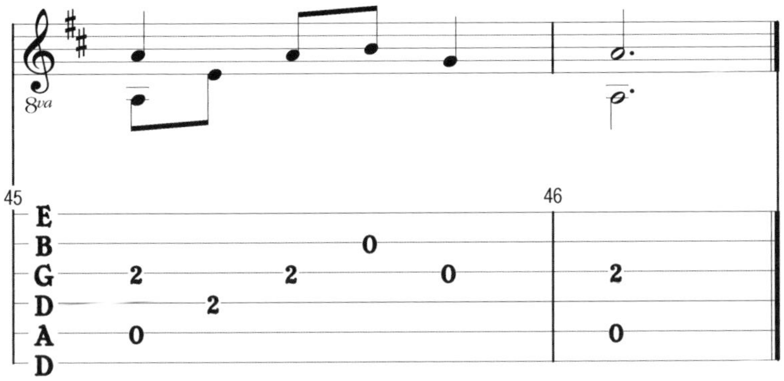

8

Rose of Allendale

Dropped-D Tuning

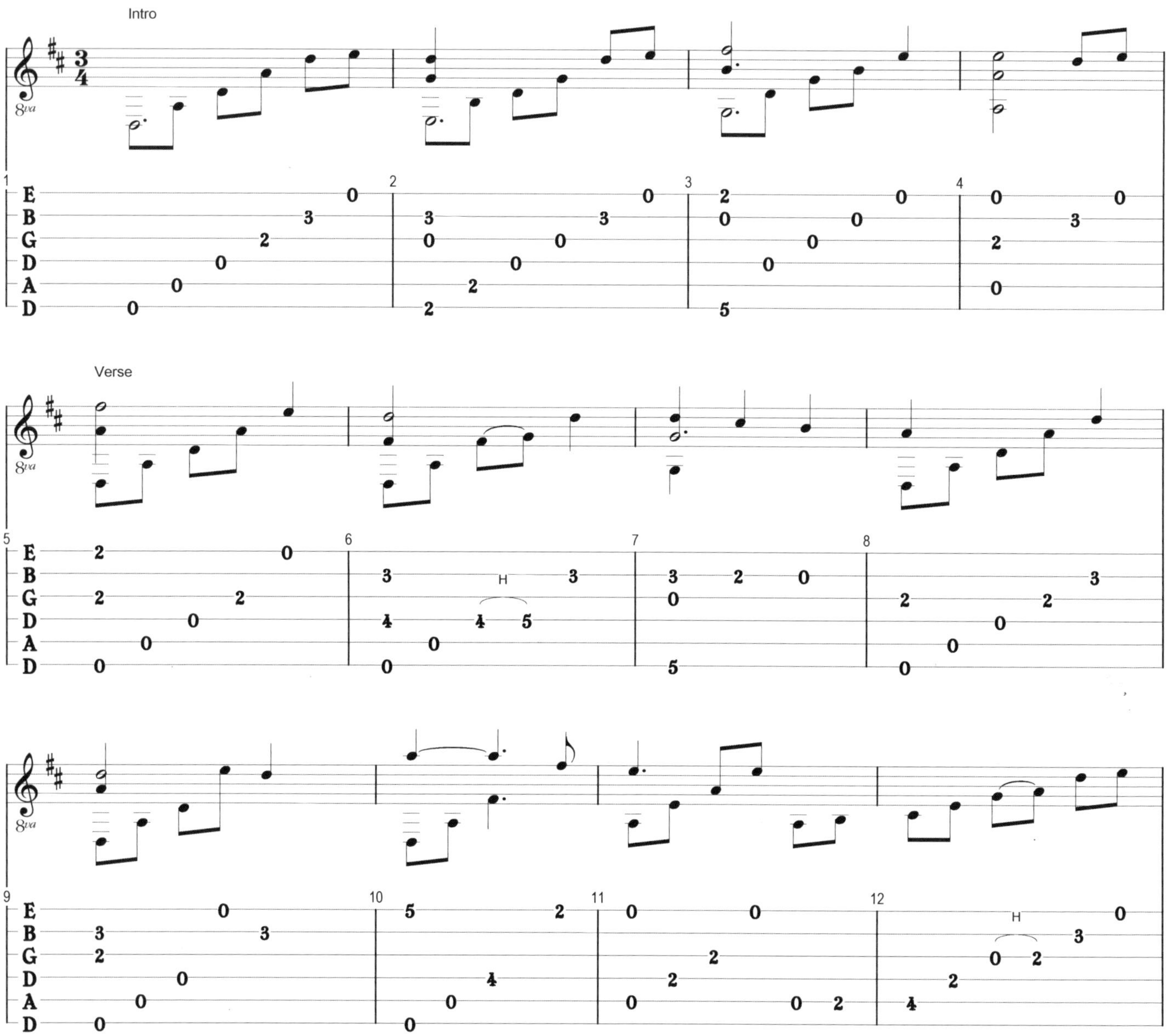

Rose of Allendale (Page 2/4)

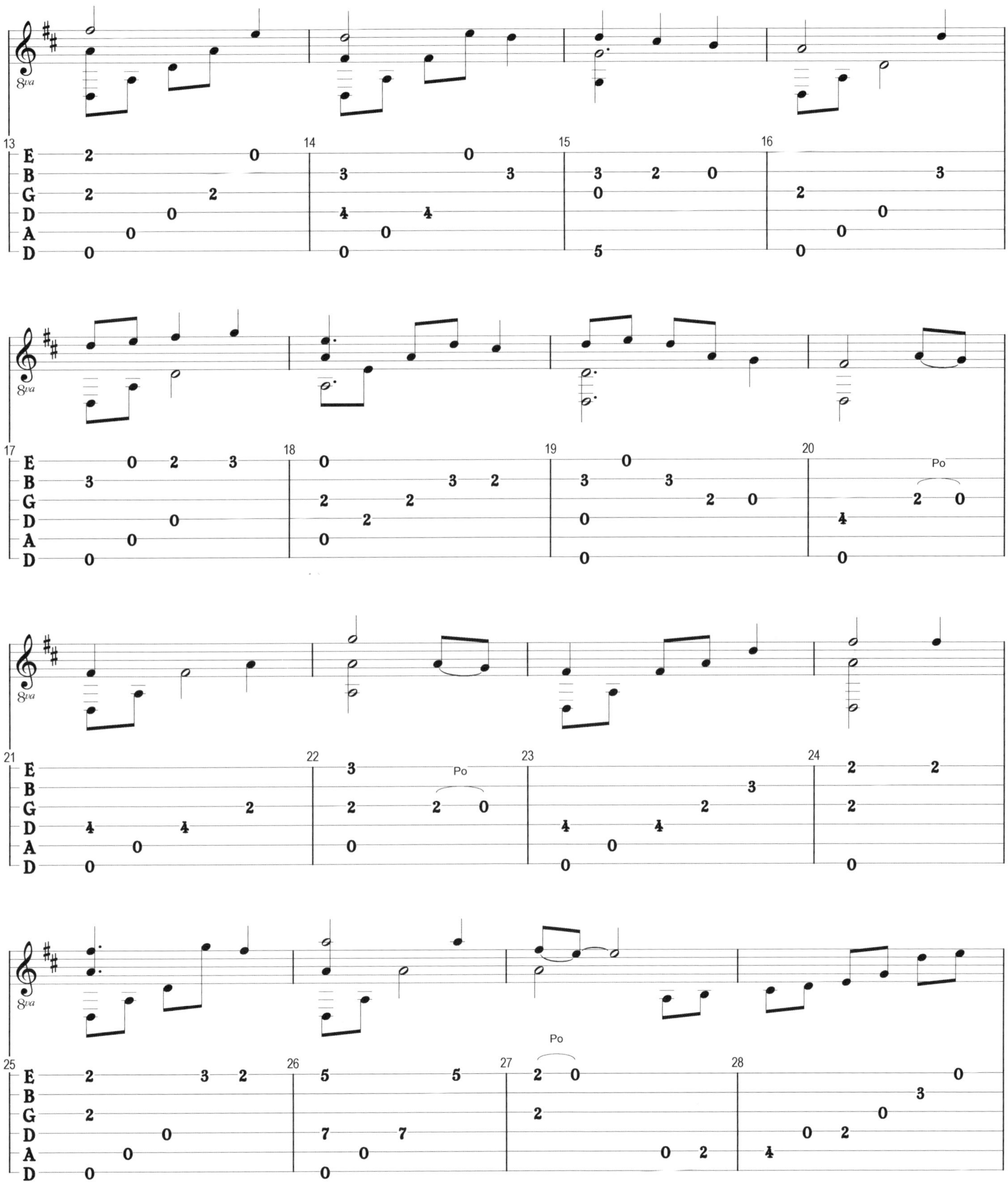

Rose of Allendale (Page 3/4)

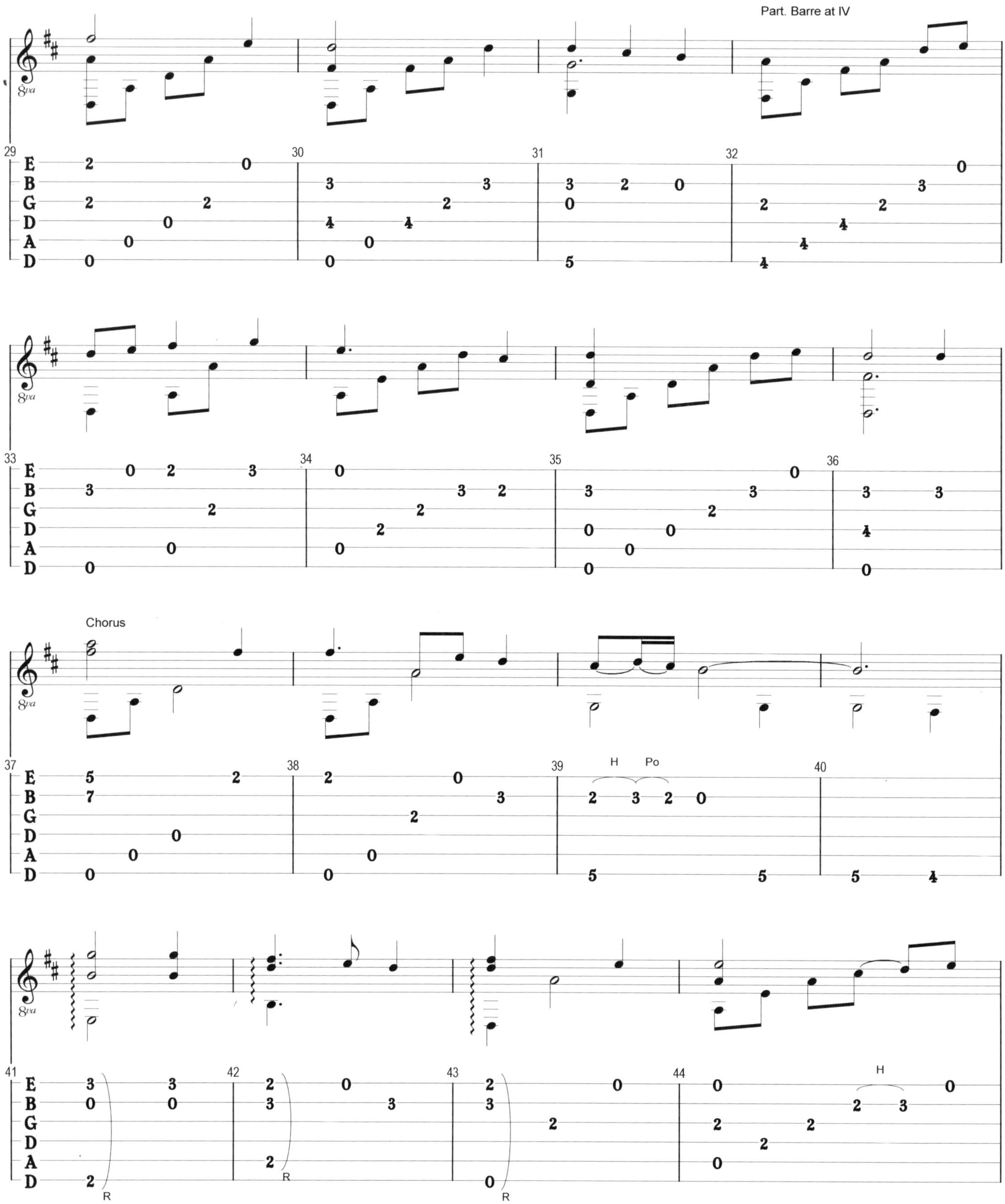

Rose of Allendale (Page 4/4)

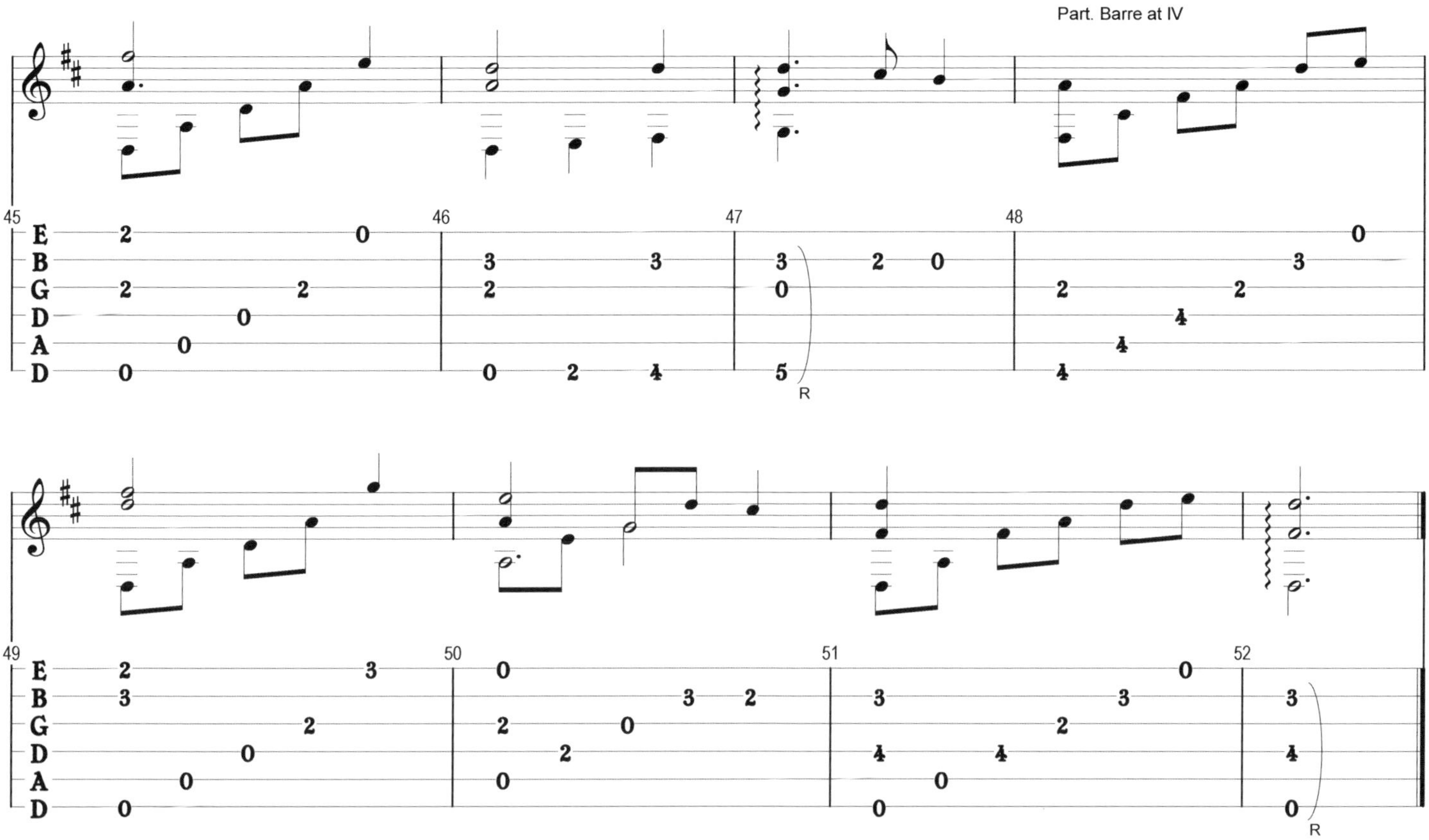

Once in A Blue Moon

9

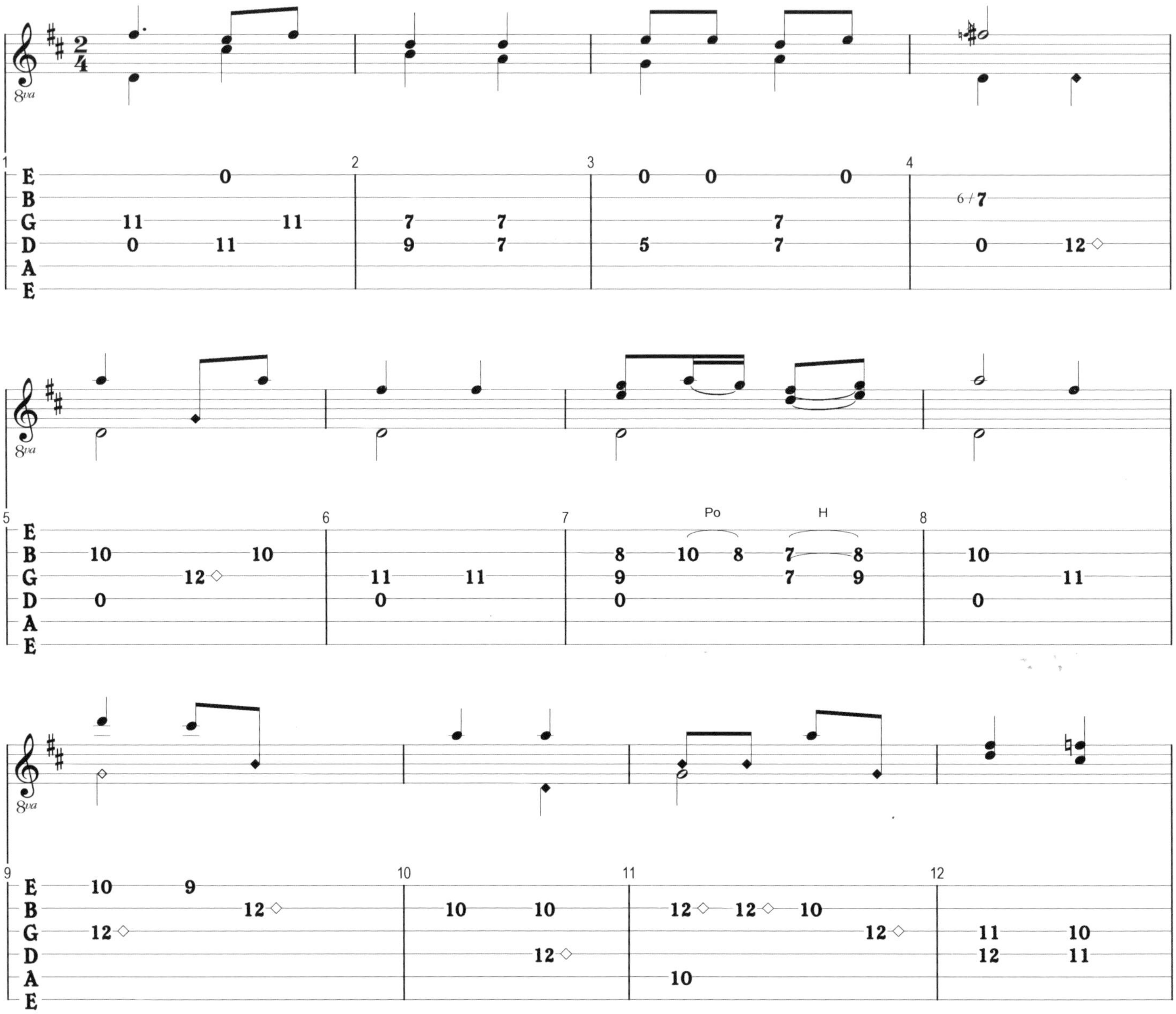

Once in A Blue Moon (Page 2/5)

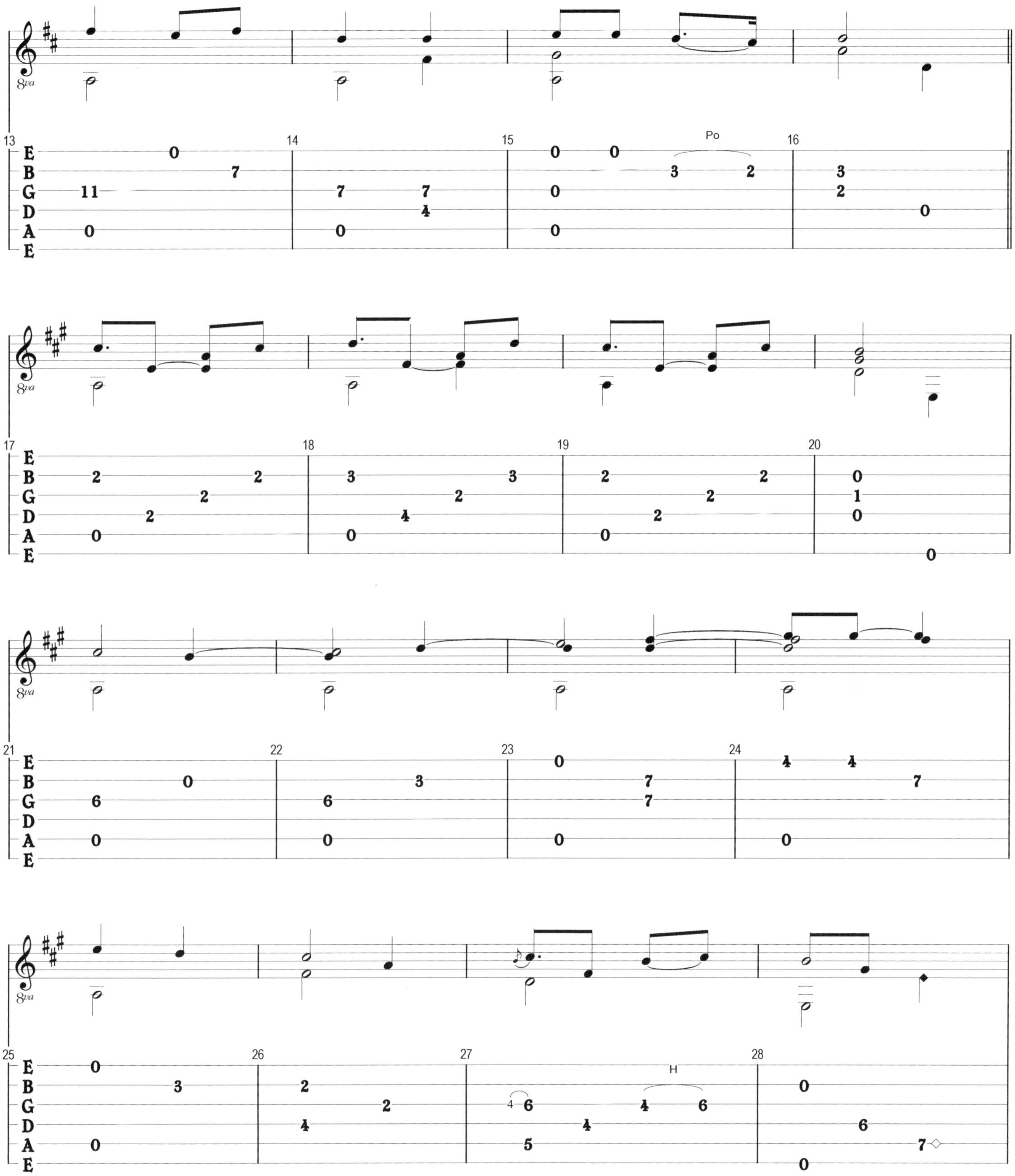

Once in A Blue Moon (Page 3/5)

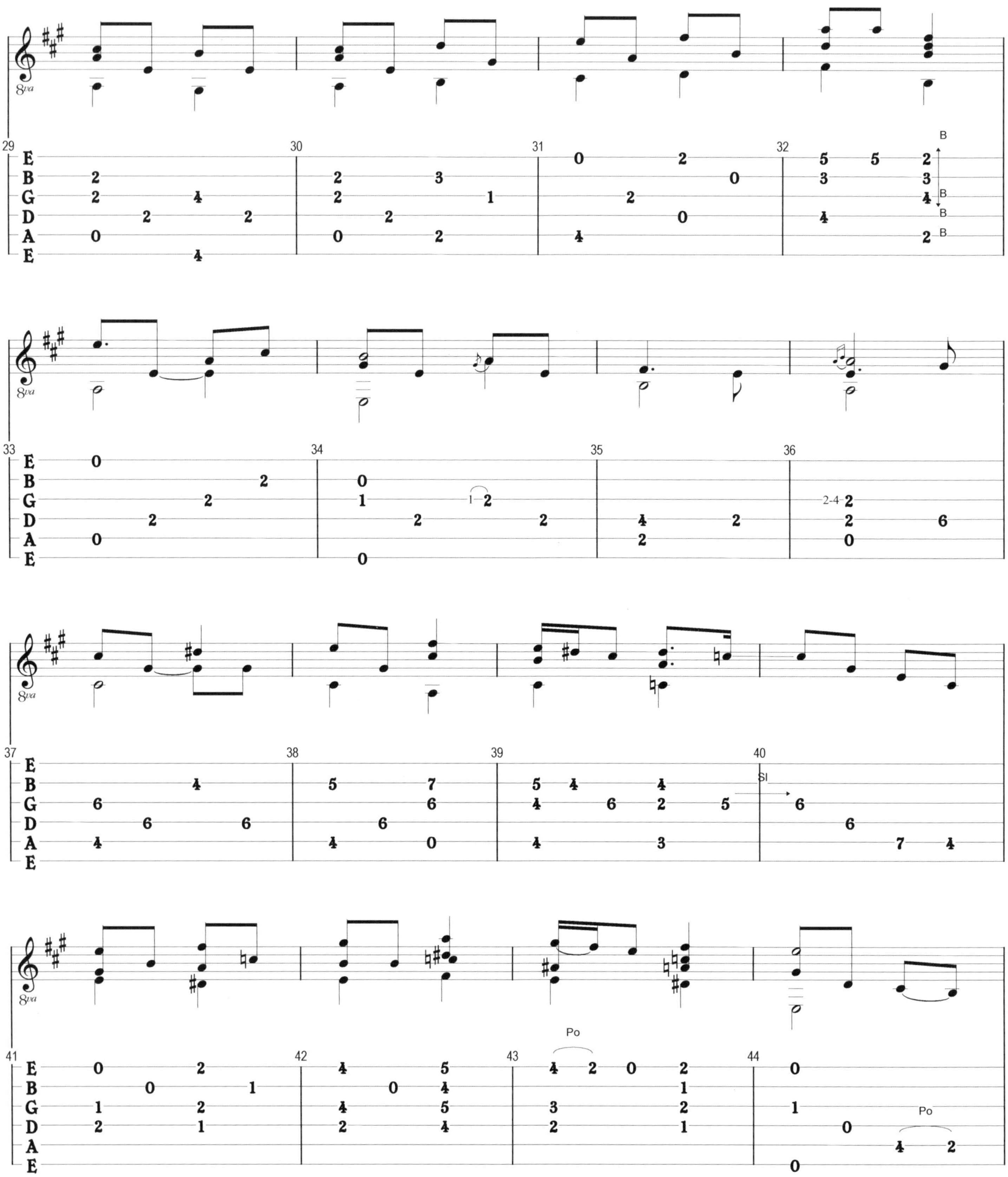

Once in A Blue Moon (Page 4/5)

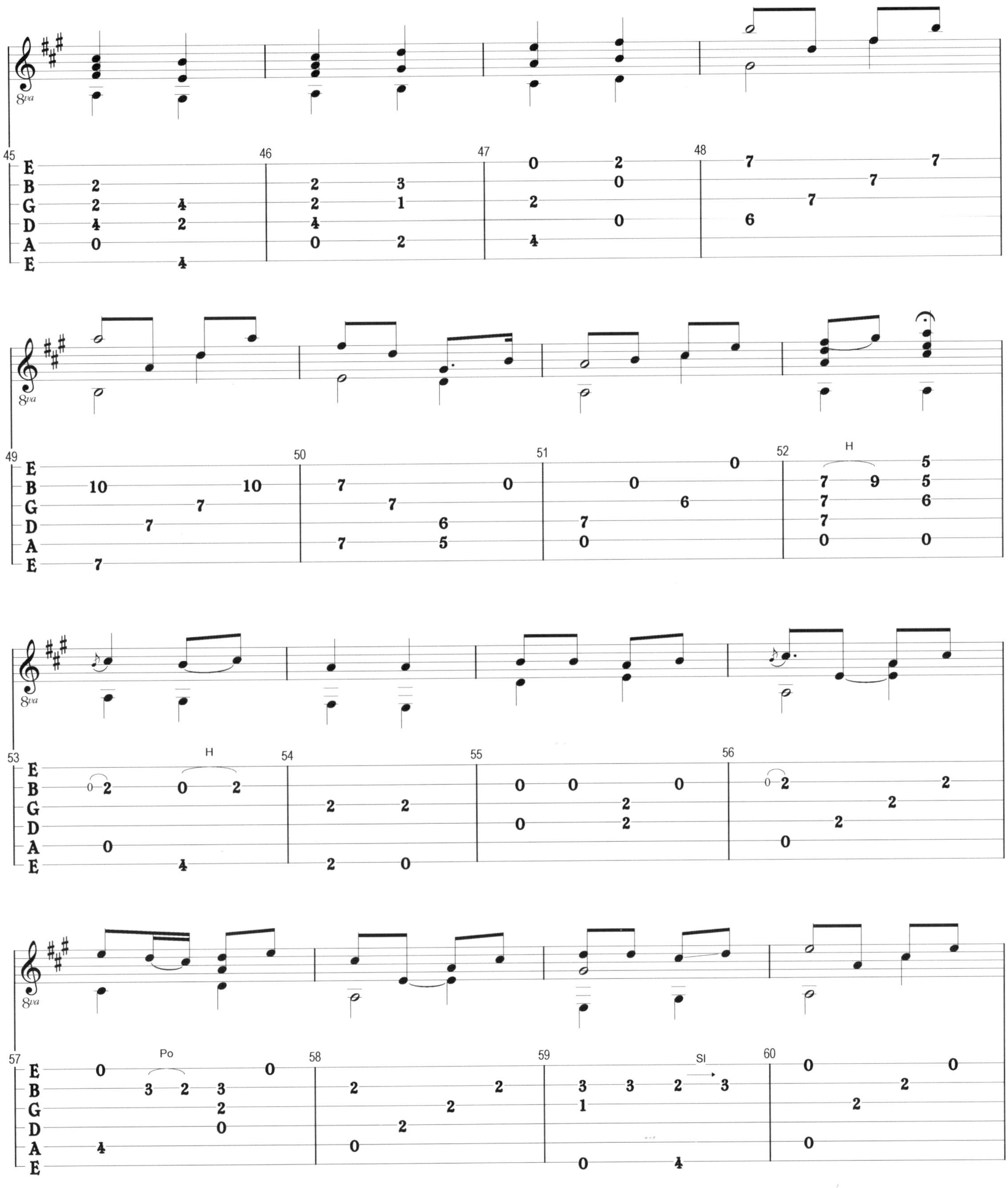

Once in A Blue Moon (Page 5/5)

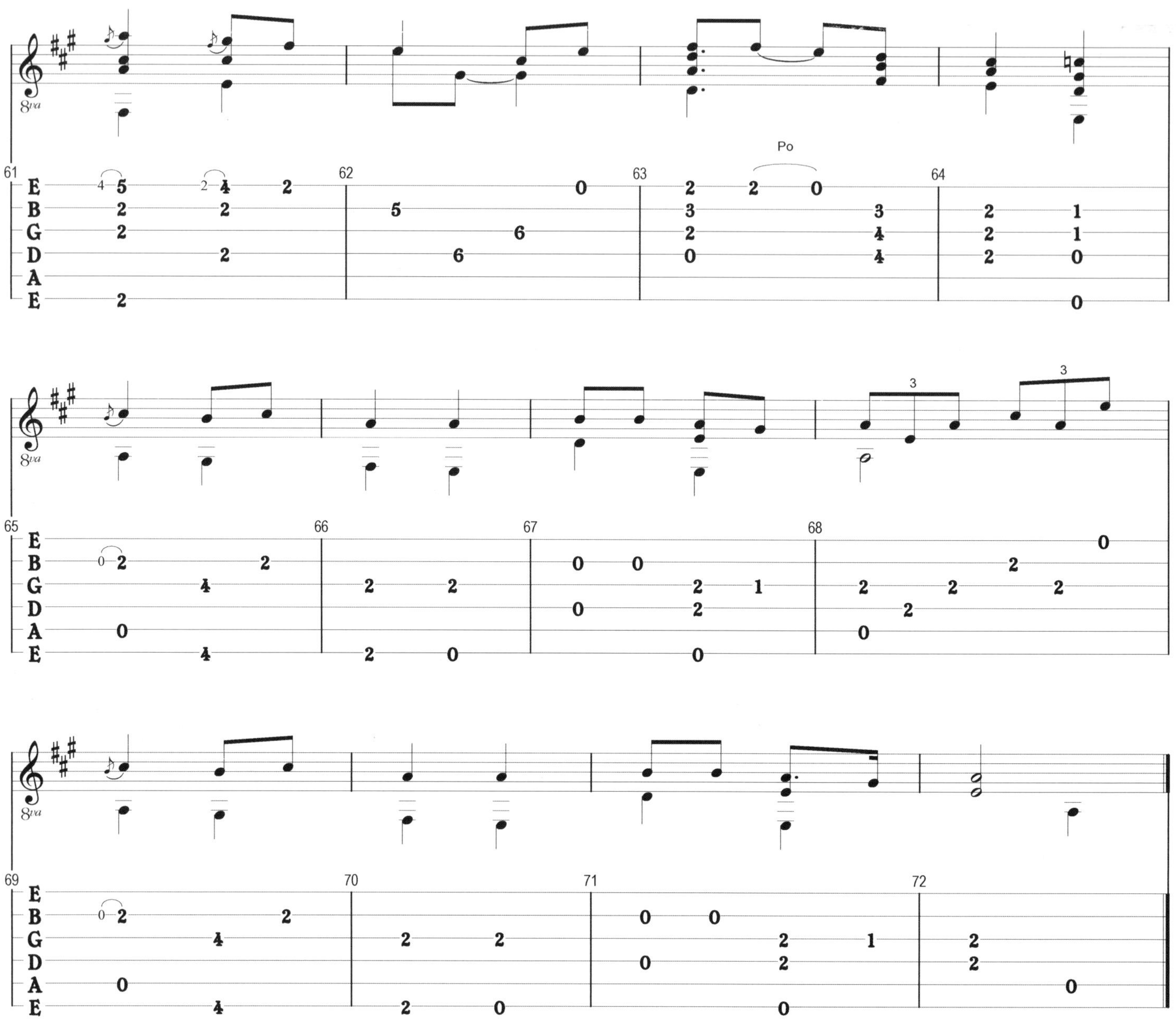